KNOWLEDGE ENCYCLOPEDIA

ELECTRONICS & COMMUNICATIONS

INVENTIONS & DISCOVERIES

(An imprint of Prakash Books Pvt. Ltd.)

Wonder House Books
Corporate & Editorial Office
113-A, 1st Floor, Ansari Road,
Daryaganj, New Delhi-110002
Tel +91 11 2324 7062-65

Printed in 2020 in India

ISBN : 9789390391431

Table of Contents

BREAKTHROUGHS IN ELECTRONICS AND COMMUNICATION

Can you imagine your life in the absence of modern-day labour-saving gizmos and tech-powered entertainment? Amazingly though, electronics have been around for just over 100 years. This is no more than a blip in the long, long timeline of human existence.

Great leaps in technology—particularly in communications—were made during the many wars of the previous century. In fact, you would be surprised by just how much scientists, spies and undercover agents have in common! Our treasured gadgets may have started out as a means for sending secret codes across oceans, or as pure scientific curiosity, but they have now taken over our homes, schools and workplaces. So, what are the important inventions that have become indispensable to us? Read on to find out!

▼ Budding scientists tinkering with robots

Vacuum Tubes

Did you know that you could create electricity by heating certain materials? Thomas Edison first observed this in 1875, when he was fiddling around with a light bulb. A few years later, British engineer John Ambrose Fleming used his discovery to invent the first **vacuum tube**, called a diode.

After the diode, vacuum tubes became more complex. Until a few decades ago, they were used to power lots of communication devices. This included radios, televisions and even computers.

▲ *Sir John Ambrose Fleming (1849–1945)*

How Does it Work?

Electricity is generated when lots of tiny, invisible particles called **electrons** travel across a medium. A stream of moving electrons is called an electric current. The vacuum tube behaves like an electric switch. When you turn it on, electricity will run through it. The tube looks like a glass bulb. Inside it, is a plate called the **anode**, and a filament called the **cathode**. Air is removed from the bulb, creating a **vacuum**.

If you send electricity into the cathode, it will become glowing hot and give off electrons. These electrons travel through the vacuum to the anode, creating an electric current. If you stop heating the cathode, it will stop releasing electrons, and the current will be 'switched off'.

▼ *A vacuum tube with a glowing cathode filament*

Modern Uses of Vacuum Tubes

Vacuum-tube technology is rarely used in the 21st century, as it has become obsolete. Nevertheless, there are a handful of applications for this gadget. Vacuum tubes are used in high-quality stereo systems. These stereo systems are used by music professionals and sound technicians.

Vacuum tubes are also used in instruments such as electric guitars. They have vacuum-tube amplifiers. Similarly, fluorescent displays are often thin vacuum-tube displays used to convey simple information in audio and video equipment. X-ray machines, radars and even microwave ovens sometimes are fitted with vacuum tubes.

▲ *A modern sound amplifier with vacuum tubes*

⊛ Incredible Individuals

JJ Thompson was the son of an English bookseller. He revolutionised the world of physics by discovering the electron. For this, he received a Nobel Prize in 1906 and was knighted by King Edward VII in 1908.

Semiconductors and Microchips

Vacuum tubes were known to be bulky and breakable. Thus, early electronic machines took up a lot of space and needed frequent repair. During 1947–1948, three Americans—John Bardeen, Walter Brattain and William Shockley—invented the **transistor**, which replaced vacuum tubes in electronics. This is because the transistor was small and sturdy, required very little power and released very little heat.

🔍 Semiconductors

A transistor is made primarily of silicon, a substance found in sand and glass. Silicon is a **semiconductor**. This means that the way it **conducts** electricity can be changed by adding other materials to it.

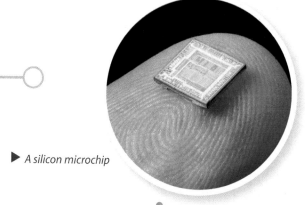

▶ *A silicon microchip*

🔍 Microchips

The first transistors were used to make lighter machines, like portable radios and hearing aids. During the 1960s and 70s, scientists began to draw tiny electric circuits on to silicon chips. This created Integrated Circuits (IC), also called **microchips**. These circuits acted like wires to conduct electricity.

These days, a single microchip—which is smaller than the tip of your finger—can hold thousands of transistors. They are used to make everything, from toasters and phones to super-computers and robots.

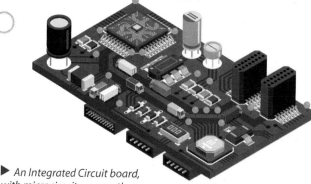

▶ *An Integrated Circuit board, with microcircuits connecting different parts of the board*

👤 In Real Life

The first proper digital computer, Electronic Numerical Integrator and Computer (ENIAC), was built during World War II. It weighed 30,000 kilograms, used 18,000 vacuum tubes and gave off a lot of heat! This massive machine occupied an entire basement, where it was arranged in the shape of the letter U along three walls.

◀ *Experts operating the gargantuan ENIAC, 1946*

Batteries

A battery stores electrical energy in chemical form. In the year 1800, Italian physicist Alessandro Volta invented the first modern battery. Volta arranged zinc and copper plates in a pile, like a stack of coins. In between the plates, he placed pieces of vinegar- or brine-soaked leather, or pasteboard. This was the first structure that allowed scientists to store and use electricity in a controlled manner.

Volta's battery is called the voltaic cell. Today, there are many varieties of batteries. Some are single-use (primary batteries) while others are rechargeable (secondary batteries).

▲ A voltaic cell (1801)

▲ A Lithium-ion battery

🔍 Commonly-used Batteries

Lithium-ion batteries are so light and small, they are called cells. They are rechargeable, long-lasting, environment-friendly and used in phones and computers. You can even use solar power (that is, the sun's energy) to recharge these cells.

Big rectangular lead-acid batteries are fitted into car engines. They are used to start the car and power its air-conditioner, radio, GPS and other devices. These batteries last up to four years on an average.

AA and AAA batteries are most commonly used in remote controls, headphones, clocks and portable players. The AA batteries are slightly larger and stronger than the AAA batteries.

Most of our watches run on small alkaline batteries that are cost-effective and easily available. However, expensive watches use cells that contain lithium or silver oxide—these are much more reliable.

🔍 Disposing Used Batteries

Many batteries contain toxic chemicals that can leak out and affect you and your surroundings. Lead and cadmium, for instance, can stunt growth, lower the IQ, cause breathing and digestion problems and even cancer. So, deposit the used batteries at a recycling unit, where experts can safely get rid of harmful chemicals.

▶ Used batteries should be given to a recycling unit for safe disposal and not chucked away like regular dry garbage

Calculators

The first calculators were mechanical, not electrical. They were simple wooden frames with rows of beads, representing 10s, 100s and 1000s. This invention was called an abacus and used as far back as in 2000 BCE in ancient Egypt.

In the 17th century, a new type of calculator called the slide rule was invented. This contained different scales that could slide against each other to do multiplications, divisions and other arithmetic calculations. For the next 300 years, this was the most popular calculator in use. In the 19th century, inventors continued to make mechanical calculating machines that became smaller and easier to use.

▲ Students learning how to use an abacus

Electrical Calculators

Today's digital calculators are based on a machine called the 'arithmometer', invented by French mathematician Blaise Pascal in 1642. In the mid-1950s, electronic data processing gave rise to the first electronic calculators. By the late 20th century, they could perform arithmetic that most mathematicians could not solve using pen and paper.

▲ Arithmometers sat on your desk like old typewriters

Nowadays, calculators have memory space and are programmable like computers. Indeed, most calculators come inbuilt into your phone and computer.

◄ The Curta Calculator, 1948

◄ Modern calculators come with keys for unique arithmetic functions. Some are so sophisticated, they are powered by solar cells

⊛ Incredible Individuals

The first portable calculator was also a mechanical device. It was invented by Austrian engineer Curt Herzstark during World War II. Herzstark was arrested by the Nazis for being Jewish. He was sent to the Buchenwald Concentration Camp. However, he was so knowledgeable and skilled, the Nazis spared his life, but continued to exploit his intellect.

Solar Energy

Do you know the meaning of the word 'photovoltaic'?
It refers to converting light into electrical energy.
Sunlight (or solar energy) can thus be turned into
electricity. This is an amazing alternative to other forms
of energy, as it reduces pollution and is renewable.

Solar Cells

The sun's energy is converted into electrical energy by small devices called
solar cells. Thousands of cells are arrayed to form panels. Large groups
of panels are then used as power stations. They distribute electricity to
factories, offices and homes. People can even install solar panels on their
rooftops to harness solar energy for their homes.

Renewable, Clean Energy

Conventional energy sources, like wood, coal, petrol and nuclear materials,
leave toxic waste every time they are used. In comparison, solar energy
is clean, as it generates no refuse and does not harm your health or the
environment. There is also an endless supply of this energy.

1954

Darryl Chapin, Calvin
Fuller and Gerald
Pearson patent a way
of using silicon in
solar cells.

1905

Albert Einstein
publishes his paper
on the photoelectric
effect and the theory
of relativity. He wins
the Nobel Prize for
his findings, in 1921.

▲ *Albert Einstein*

1839

Alexandre
Becquerel
discovers the
photovoltaic
effect.

1860–90s

French mathematician
August Mouchet and
his assistant, Abel Pifre,
construct the first solar-
powered engines.

1891

American inventor
Clarence Kemp
patents the first
commercial solar
water heater.

▲ *Alexandre Becquerel*

The Solar Timeline

1955

Solar cells begin to be made for commercial use. Early products include money-changers and devices that decode computers of the era.

Mid-1950s

Architect Frank Bridgers designs the first office building using that uses solar water heating.

◀ *Solar panels on a satellite*

1981

Paul MacCready flies the first solar-powered aircraft called the Solar Challenger from France to England. The Challenger has over 16,000 solar cells on its wings.

1963

Japan installs a 242-watt, photovoltaic array on a lighthouse.

1958

Vanguard I becomes the first space satellite to use a solar array to power its radios. In the same year, Explorer III, Vanguard II and Sputnik 3 are all launched with solar-powered systems. Even today, this is the accepted energy source for space applications.

1982

Hans Tholstrup drives the Quiet Achiever (the first solar-powered car) between Sydney and Perth in Australia. It proves to be far more efficient than the first gasoline-powered car.

▲ *Recharge station of a solar powered car*

2000

Astronauts begin installing solar panels on the International Space Station in the largest array ever seen in space. There are 32,800 cells in each 'wing' of the array.

▲ *The International Space Station*

1983

The first stand-alone home to be powered by solar cells is built in the Hudson River Valley, USA.

▲ *Solar panel on a house roof*

Telegraph

The telegraph was the first electric as well as the first wireless technology that allowed us to send long-distance messages quickly. In the early 1800s, electricity was still new. At this time, two Germans—Carl Gauss and Wilhelm Weber—built the first real electric telegraph. However, this machine could not send messages beyond 1 kilometre. During this period, other inventors came up with their own versions of the telegraph, but none of them really took off.

▲ *An illustration of an old telegraph office (1867)*

🔍 Samuel Morse and the Code

In the 1830s, American inventor Samuel FB Morse invented a system of dots and dashes to match the English alphabet. This system, called the Morse Code, made it easy to telegraph messages on a new model that he developed. In 1843, Morse was asked by the American government to build a 60-km-long telegraph system. Public use of this first telegraph line began on 24th May, 1844, with Morse sending the message, "What hath God wrought!" By 1851, the USA had over 50 telegraph companies.

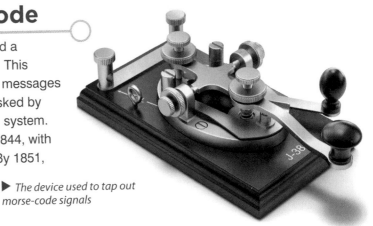

▶ *The device used to tap out morse-code signals*

🔍 Radio Waves and the Wireless Telegraph

In 1888, a German physicist named Heinrich Hertz discovered that it was possible to transmit electrical energy through the air. This energy travelled in invisible waves and eventually came to be called **radio waves**.

Over 1894–1896, Italian scientist Guglielmo Marconi experimented with various ways of sending signals in Morse Code using radio waves. By 1906, he had refined his system so well, he was able to send messages across the Atlantic Ocean. He is thus the inventor of the wireless telegraph.

◀ *A telegraph operator sending messages by tapping them out in Morse code*

▼ *A stamp featuring Guglielmo Marconi, who won the Nobel Prize for Physics in 1909. His discoveries in wireless communication are the basis for our modern understanding of long-distance radio*

Radio

In the early 1900s, Canadian engineer Reginald Fessenden was able to combine sound from a microphone with a type of electromagnetic wave to send messages over long distances. These electromagnetic waves are now called radio waves and are used by many devices other than the radio, including TV and mobile phones.

Fessenden made the first ever public radio broadcast in America on the eve of Christmas in 1904. He played 'O Holy Night' on his violin and could be heard by ships that were 160 kilometres away. However, regular public broadcasting only began in 1920.

⭐ Incredible Individuals

In 1938, Orson Welles rewrote *The War of the Worlds* (a book about Martians invading Earth) as a radio drama. Broadcast as a Halloween special, the drama began with a series of fake news bulletins. The bulletins lasted an hour and seemed so real that many people believed they were truly being attacked by aliens. Entire cities became hysterical and were thrown into a turmoil!

▲ *Reginald Fessenden, the inventor of the radio, a photo from c. 1906*

🔍 The Early Days of Radio

All radio systems since then have worked using a transmitter that sends sound signals, and a receiver, which finds the signal and lets us hear radio programmes. Nowadays, radio broadcasting happens over two main types of channels: **AM** and **FM**.

AM channels can be heard over thousands of miles and are usually used to broadcast news, sports and talk shows. FM channels offer better sound quality and are more popular. They travel shorter distances and are used by local police, taxis, and other groups to listen to information, music and entertainment shows.

Surprisingly, when you listen to a live concert on the radio, the music reaches you faster than it does a person in the actual concert hall. This is because your radio transmits sound to you in the form of electric signals at the speed of light. In contrast, sound waves (the vibrations made by a voice or instrument) travel more slowly through the air to reach the person in the hall.

▲ *An electronic survey system of radio transmitters and monitors*

▼ *A radio from the 1950s*

👤✓ In Real Life

If you have an AM radio, you can tap the terminal of a nine-volt battery with a coin to create radio waves! Switch on the radio and turn the dial till you hear static (steady crackling noises). While holding the battery near the radio's antenna, quickly tap the two terminals on the battery, so they are connected for an instant. Try this fun trick and you will be able to hear the radio waves.

▶ *A 9-volt battery*

Television
Moving Pictures
Sent on Radio Waves

All TVs need three things to function. These are the TV camera, which turns sound and picture into a signal; the TV transmitter, which sends the signal using radio waves; and the TV set at home (the receiver), which turns the signal back into image and sound.

Broadcasting and Cable

The earliest TV broadcasts were seen—mostly by scientists—in the late 1920s. But by the 1950s, there was steady public interest in TV shows. Cable TV was invented around this time and it streamed many more channels than regular radio transmission was able to. It took around 30 years for cable TV to be accepted around the world! These days, TVs use satellite dishes as transmitters and receivers to provide high-definition, high-quality programmes.

▼ *A film strip showing a sequence of still shots from the Trinity Test, the first nuclear explosion conducted by humans*

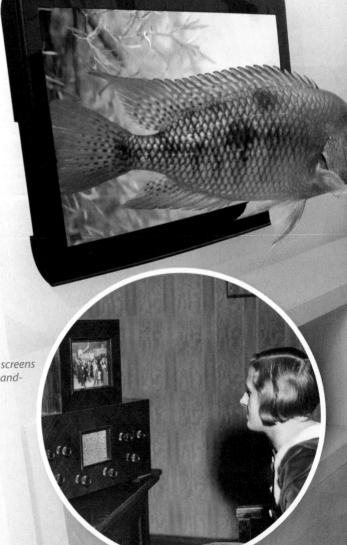

In Real Life

The first TVs could only stream black-and-white content. Much later, engineers discovered that any colour can be made by mixing the three primary colours: red, green and blue. Eventually, inventors made cameras that could capture separate red, green and blue signals; transmission systems that could beam colour signals; and TV sets that could turn them into multicoloured images.

▶ *The first TVs had tiny screens and showed only black-and-white images*

Some Brilliant Minds behind the TV

In the 1880s, people were thinking, if voices can be sent over the air, why not pictures? In 1884, German inventor Paul Nipkow used spinning discs with small holes in them to break up images into smaller elements. He was then able to recombine these into a black-and-white image. In 1906, Boris Rosing of Russia combined Nipkow's disc with the Cathode Ray Tube (CRT) to develop the first basic TV set. In 1931, the spinning disc was once and for all replaced by the electronic camera, invented by another Russian, Vladimir Zworykin.

◀ *John Logie Baird with his television receiver*

Flat Screen TVs and 3D Technology

With the invention of LCD, plasma screen and OLED technologies, TVs became as flat as the walls they are mounted on. LCD and plasma TVs have millions of tiny picture elements called pixels, which give us sharp images. OLED TVs use electricity to generate light particles called **photons** to display even better images.

Nowadays, engineers are trying to bring images out of the screen and into 'real' space. You may have seen this in movie halls when you're given glasses to watch 3D movies. There is still a long way to go for this technology with many exciting inventions to come.

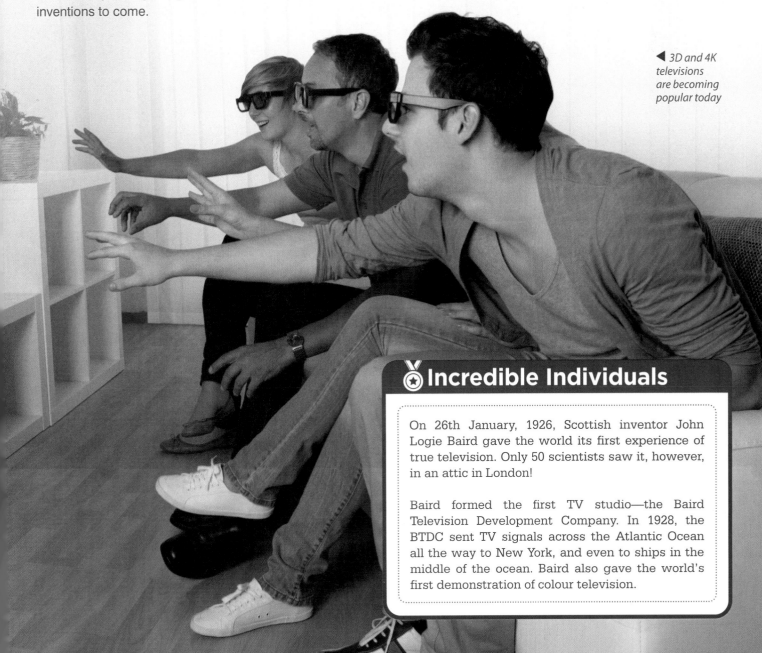

◀ *3D and 4K televisions are becoming popular today*

ⓥ Incredible Individuals

On 26th January, 1926, Scottish inventor John Logie Baird gave the world its first experience of true television. Only 50 scientists saw it, however, in an attic in London!

Baird formed the first TV studio—the Baird Television Development Company. In 1928, the BTDC sent TV signals across the Atlantic Ocean all the way to New York, and even to ships in the middle of the ocean. Baird also gave the world's first demonstration of colour television.

Who Invented the Telephone?

Most people think that the telephone was invented by Alexander Graham Bell in 1876. But nobody knows the amazing story behind the real inventor! In 1841, Italian inventor Antonio Meucci had already designed a telephone. He applied to the government for recognition in 1871. But the officials stalled and ignored him.

◀ *Bell's first telephone was called the Centennial Model because it was first seen by the public on 25th June, 1876 at the Centennial Exhibition in Philadelphia, USA*

▼ *An old battery-operated phone*

▲ *A wooden telephone from the late 19th century*

▶ *Early tall telephones were called candlesticks*

⚡ Isn't It Amazing!

The first words Bell ever spoke over the telephone were to his assistant. He said, "Mr. Watson, come here. I want to see you."

The Full Story

Bell shared a lab with Meucci at this time. In 1876, he also wrote to the government about the same invention. This time, the officials responded, and he became rich and famous! A furious Meucci sued Bell for fraud. But Meucci was an old man by then. He died before he could win the case. In 2002, well over a century later, the US Congress acknowledged Meucci's contributions.

American professor Elisha Gray also developed a telephone. It is suggested that he filed for government recognition on the same day as Alexander Graham Bell! The date was 14th February, 1876. Records show that Bell was the fifth person to file a notice that day. Gray was the 39th. Rather than investigate Gray's claims, the Patent Office simply named Bell the inventor of the telephone.

▲ *Elisha Gray*

Battery-operated Phones

Early phones did not rely on the phone company for electricity. They had a built-in magneto, which used a coil and a magnet-generated electric current. To use these phones, you first "recharged" the battery by cranking up a lever on its right side. If you did not do this, the phone at the other end would not ring.

◀ *The first cordless phone was invented in 1962 for the World Fair in Seattle, USA*

⭐ Incredible Individuals

The first phone book suggested a cheery 'hulloa' as a greeting. Bell thought 'Ahoy' was a better option. It was Thomas Edison who made 'Hello' the standard phone greeting.
To end the call, the phone book suggested 'God be with you', which got shortened to 'goodbye' and 'bye-bye'.

▼ *Candlestick phones soon gave way to rotary-dial and push-button telephones*

Cell Phones
Old Technology for a Modern Invention

Do you know how cell phones work? They use batteries and radio waves. When you make a call, your phone uses FM radio waves to signal the nearest antenna tower. The tower then sends your signal forward to a central tower, which in turn connects you to the landline or cell phone you are calling.

In most places, a tower can receive signals from around 25–26 square kilometres. This area is called a cell; and this is why your phone is called a cell phone. As you travel, towers from different cells forward the signal.

🔍 SIM Card

If you open the back of your phone, you will see that it holds a battery and a shiny small card. This is called the SIM card. It became a part of cell phones in the early 1990s. The SIM is a microchip that holds all your identification and security details. Even if your phone gets damaged, you can put this chip into another phone and get back some of your contacts and text messages. The smallest SIM card in use today is called a Nano-SIM.

▲ The SIM card being inserted into a phone

▲ The microchip side of the SIM

🔍 Smartphones

The first semblance of smartphones came out in the 1990s. These were the IBM Simon and the Nokia Communicator 9000. The first real smartphone came out in 2000—the Ericsson R380. It was followed by phones like the Palm and BlackBerry, which were hugely successful. In 2007, Apple revolutionised smartphones by releasing the iPhone—the first phone to use a touchscreen instead of buttons. This technology has been popular ever since.

◀ *Ericsson R380, Nokia Communicator and a Blackberry phone*

🔍 Operating Systems

Smartphones these days are as smart as computers. So, they need an Operating System (OS) to do their work. The three major OSs used in smartphones are Android (by Google), iOS (by Apple) and Windows (by Microsoft). Just because two phones run the same OS doesn't mean the phones are the same. There are physical differences such as weight and screen size. The speed of the phone and its memory can also vary. And there may be differences in software, as phone-makers load different programmes and apps on to phones.

▲ *These logos of the three giants of the smartphone industry, Microsoft, Android and Apple, represent some of the most popular brands today*

👤 In Real Life

Our smartphones are now so capable and well-connected, they can interact with reality. For instance, apps can use data from satellites in the sky to tell us about our surroundings in real time. You can simply point your phone at the road ahead of you, and the app will show you bits of information about it, along with the route ahead. You can find fun new places and even play games like Pokemon Go with such augmented reality.

▶ *iPhone—the first phone to use a touchscreen instead of buttons*

Indispensable Office Technology

A photocopier is a machine that can reproduce text or images on paper by using light, heat, chemicals and electricity. The first of its kind was developed in America in 1937 by the physicist Chester Carlson. Most modern offices use photocopiers. These are also called Xerox machines, after the most commonly known photocopier brand.

Inside the machine is a light-sensitive surface covered with ink (or toner). When light passes through the paper that is being copied, the ink is sprayed on another sheet, forming a copy of the original. Electric charges are used on the ink and the copy paper to ensure the ink sticks to the new sheet. Finally, heat is applied to fuse the ink on to the paper.

▲ A photocopier in a library

🔍 Printer

We all know printers as machines that print documents from a computer. Most printers these days are non-impact devices. This means that they form images using a matrix of tiny dots. The most popular variety of printers is the **laser** printer. It was invented in the 1960s by an engineer named Gary Starkweather.

The laser printer uses a beam of laser light to etch images on a light-conducting drum. The image is then carried from the drum on to paper using electric photocopying. Another popular non-impact printer is the inkjet printer, invented in 1976. This works by spraying electrically charged ink drops directly on to the print paper.

▲ An inkjet printer

💡 Isn't It Amazing!

The earliest form of printing began in 8th-century China and Korea. People would carve pages of books on to flat wooden blocks. They would then apply ink to the blocks and press them on to sheets of paper. This is how books were made for hundreds of years.

▶ A modern laser printer

⭐ Incredible Individuals

In the 15th century, a German goldsmith called Johannes Gutenberg invented the printing press. This was the first machine capable of making multiple copies of pages. The printing press made it faster, easier and more cost-effective to produce books. This, in turn, allowed all people—not just the rich—to acquire an education. Now that people could read, novels and newspapers became popular.

▲ *Cartridges of a colour printer*

🔍 Fax

The fax machine, also called telefax and facsimile, is a machine that uses wires and radio waves to send and receive messages. These machines scan text or art off paper and transmit the information across phone lines to other machines, where the original document is reproduced on paper.

Over the 19th and 20th centuries, many inventors created and modified this invention. Modern fax machines are cheap, reliable, fast and easy to use. They almost replaced telegraphic services in offices and homes. They are used as a quick alternative to postal services and couriers.

▲ *A fax machine*

Computers: A Fruit of the Loom

The idea of a computer first came from weaving. In 1801, French merchant Joseph Jaquard developed the industrial loom. This machine could weave detailed images on to cloth. Images were stored as punched patterns on cards. Each row of holes was used for a row of threads in the pattern. About 2000 punch cards were needed for one complete image.

◀ *A used punch card*

In Real Life

In order to aid the census process, Herman Hollerith built the Tabulating Machine Company. This was later renamed to International Business Machines or IBM. Today, IBM is one of the leaders in making all things computer-related.

The Personal Computer

Until the 1970s, most people had never come across a computer. At this time, there were two types of computers. One was the large, room-sized version that cost hundreds of thousands of dollars. The other was a mass-produced mini-computer that also cost thousands of dollars and was used in laboratories and offices. The idea that everyone could have a computer at home—let alone a laptop—was considered a tall tale. What made this possible was the invention of the microprocessor. The processor is what allows the computer to make calculations instantly and respond to your commands. Lots of machines have them today—cars, dishwashers, TVs, etc. But the processor of your computer is a great deal more powerful.

The Future of Computing

In the Internet-linked 21st century, computers are getting smaller and microprocessors more powerful. In a few years, nano-computers could be small enough to fit inside your body to track your health, enhance your abilities and help you control your surroundings. Experts are already creating environments that are fully computer-controlled. This means your home, car, clothing and appliances will all respond to your signals. The exciting new field that is powering these possibilities is called quantum computing. This will use the principles of quantum theory—the study of atomic and subatomic particles—to create a new generation of super-fast computers. The full extent of its abilities is yet unimaginable.

◀ *A computer operator with a punch-card sorter at the US Census Bureau (c.1940)*

The Father of the Computer

British professor Charles Babbage realised that the punched-card system could also be used to do arithmetic. He modified the loom to create the world's first computer. It was a mechanical invention called the 'Analytical Machine'.

Inventor Herman Hollerith saw Babbage's machine and was inspired to create the 'Hollerith Desk'. The desk used punched cards to gather information from the 1890 American census. Thus, the computer moved beyond calculation to information processing.

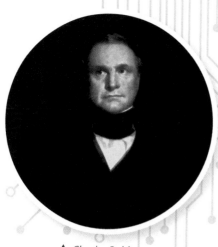
▲ *Charles Babbage*

⊛ Incredible Individuals

Ada Lovelace (1815–1852) was a mathematician and the daughter of famous British poet, Lord Byron. She met Charles Babbage in 1833. Both worked closely to further develop the computer. Among Ada's many contributions was a stepwise sequence for solving certain mathematical problems. For this amazing accomplishment, she is known as the 'world's first computer programmer'.

Ada was also the first to see the vast potential of the Analytical Engine, beyond simple number calculations. She has therefore been called the 'Prophet of the Computer Age'.

◀ *A portrait of Countess Ada Lovelace*

▼ *The 1960s electronic computer URAL-2 was located in Tashkent, Uzbekistan, and relied on vacuum tubes*

The Development of Computers

Computers have come a long way since Babbage and Lovelace first worked on them. Some countries even have super-computers to help their governments and scholars with cutting-edge research. The development of computers can be divided into three main periods.

🔍 First Generation Computers: 1937–1946

Dr John Atanasoff and Clifford Berry built the first electronic digital computer in 1937. It was called ABC (Atanasoff-Berry Computer). In 1943, the military had an electronic computer built. They called it the Colossus.

Progress was further made until, in 1946, the first general-purpose computer, the ENIAC was built. Computers of this period did one task at a time and had no operating language or systems.

◀ *The mechanism used to make precise holes on computer punch cards at the US Bureau of the Census (c.1940)*

🔍 Second Generation: 1947–1962

Computers of this period used transistors instead of vacuum tubes. In 1951, UNIVAC 1 (Universal Automatic Computer) became the first computer to be introduced to the public. The first programming languages (about 100 of them) were written for this generation of computers. Storage also became possible through devices such as disks and tapes.

▲ *UNIVAC 1 control station*

🔍 Third Generation: 1963–Present

The invention of the microchip truly revolutionised computers. They became powerful, reliable and a lot smaller. Nowadays, they can run multiple complex programmes at the same time. In 1980, the MS-DOS (Microsoft Disc Operating System) was created.

A year later, IBM introduced the personal computer or PC. Now it was possible to undertake various tasks and even play basic computer games on smaller, more affordable systems. In the 90s, Bill Gates invented the Windows operating system. With this, the PC rapidly became a part of homes and offices across the world.

⊙ Incredible Individuals

The QWERTY keyboard was created by American inventor Christopher Latham Sholes. It was first seen on 1st July, 1874.

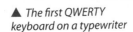

◀ *A PC from the 1990s*

▲ *The first QWERTY keyboard on a typewriter*

A Timeline of Computer and Mobile Games

1922
Steve Russell, Martin Graetz and Wayne Wiitanen design 'Spacewar!' (Widely considered the first proper computer game)

1952
Alexander Douglas, a student, designs and plays noughts and crosses on Cambridge University's EDSAC computer.

1966
Engineer Ralph Baer tries to use a TV called the 'Brown Box' to play games. It allows users to play games such as table tennis on TV, without a computer. It even had a light gun for shooting games.

1996
High-quality video cards (3dfx chipsets) are launched.

1995
Sony releases the first Play Station console.

1989
Nintendo releases Gameboy which is the first hand-held game console.

1977
Atari launches the first video game console.

1999
EverQuest is created as a Massively Multi-player Online Role-Playing Game (MMORPG).

2006
Nintendo Wii is launched. It introduces new ways of interacting with game systems.

2010
Angry Birds becomes the top-selling mobile phone game.

▲ *Controllers used in game consoles*

Digital Libraries

A computer and cell phone come with free digital space where one can save documents, movies, music, images and more. These files can also be saved on external storage devices. Pen drives, DVDs and hard discs are some examples.

Storage (sometimes called memory) is measured in **bytes**. If an external hard disc can store 1 terabyte (TB), that means it can hold about 500 hours' worth of movies. Say a book is 325-pages long; 1 TB would store 2,64,304 books. It would take a person several years to get through such a large digital library.

▼ *An audio cassette being inserted into a cassette player*

Early Storage Devices

▲ *Mark 1 William-Kilburn*

▲ *Atlas magnetic drum*

The first electronic memory device was the 1947-tested Williams-Kilburn tube. Its memory faded in seconds and had to be constantly refreshed. In 1950, the Atlas storage device was invented using a magnetic drum and a rotating cylinder coated in chemicals. This was the first type of storage good enough for public use.

New types of storage were invented throughout the 50s and 60s. These included magnetic tapes and disks, metal coils, cartridges, thin films and photo-digital storage. One notable invention was the floppy disc (or diskette). It was made by IBM in the 1970s and was popular all through the 90s.

▲ *Floppy discs*

Computer Storage

The various parts of your computer work as a team. Memory is an integral member of this team. It comes into play from the moment you turn on your computer. When you switch it on, the computer loads information from what is called Read-Only Memory (ROM). During this process, the memory controller checks that the computer's memory banks are functioning properly. Next, when you open an application, the computer looks into its Random Access Memory (RAM). The greater your RAM, the faster your computer will be. It is therefore essential not to waste RAM. Your computer will thus load only the most essential feature of an application until more is called for. When you save a file, your computer will find a more permanent memory location for it. Thus, when the application is closed, all files are removed from the RAM.

In Real Life

From 2006 onwards, you could store information online. Companies like Amazon and Dropbox made glossary-based storage available on the Internet. This was called the **Cloud**. A person could simply sign up for it, like a library membership, and store their data online.

Modern Storage: Facts

1984: The floppy disc was replaced by the CD (Compact Disc). The first CD-ROM was released by Sony and Philips. It held the *Grolier's Electronic Encyclopaedia.*

1984: Flash memory was invented by Japanese engineer, Fujio Masuoka. This allowed us to erase old, unwanted data from memory devices and replace it with new data.

1992: Experts needed smaller devices to match the ever-shrinking sizes of computers, phones and cameras. So, a company called SunDisk (later renamed SanDisk) made the first memory chip.

1995: DVDs (Digital Video Discs) were introduced. For the first time you could store an entire movie in one device.

2000: The USB flash drive (a pen drive or memory stick) was introduced.

2003: The Blu-ray disc, considered a successor of the DVD, was launched.

2009: The first 1-TB hard disc was invented.

MemoryCard

32GB Micro ⑩ SD XC

A pen drive

▲ *An external storage drive*

The Internet of Things

In 1957, the Russians launched the first man-made satellite into space. To push their own technology forward, American President Dwight Eisenhower created the Advanced Research Projects Agency (ARPA) in 1958. Over the next decade, ARPA—with some help from a company called Bolt, Beranek and Neuman (BNN)—created the first computer **network**. This was made of four different computers, running on four different operating systems, and was called ARPANET—the world's first 'Internet'.

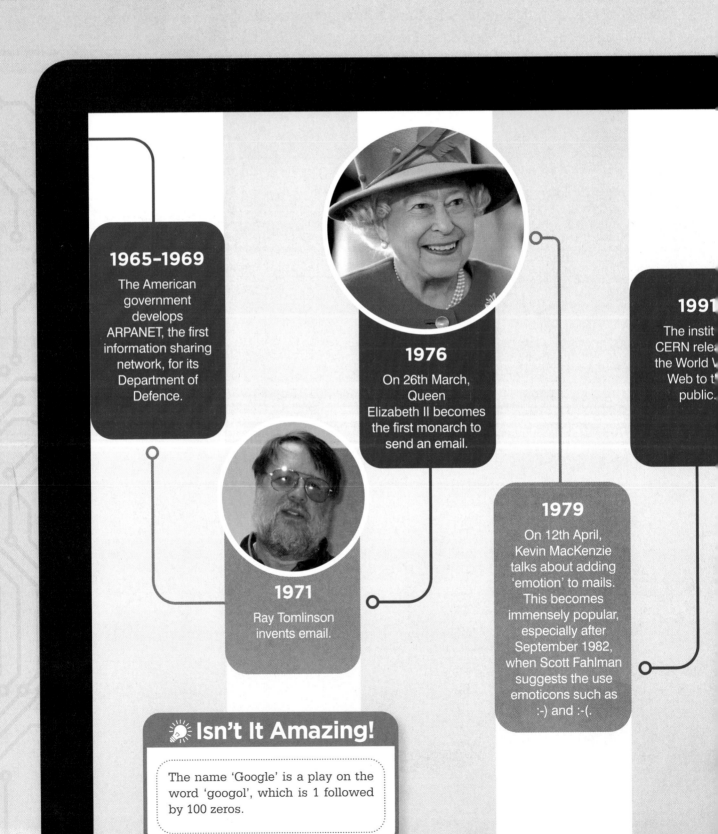

1965–1969

The American government develops ARPANET, the first information sharing network, for its Department of Defence.

1976

On 26th March, Queen Elizabeth II becomes the first monarch to send an email.

1991

The instit CERN rele the World Web to t public.

1971

Ray Tomlinson invents email.

1979

On 12th April, Kevin MacKenzie talks about adding 'emotion' to mails. This becomes immensely popular, especially after September 1982, when Scott Fahlman suggests the use emoticons such as :-) and :-(.

💡 Isn't It Amazing!

The name 'Google' is a play on the word 'googol', which is 1 followed by 100 zeros.

The Mother of the Internet

Though she didn't invent the Internet, her many, many contributions to its robust growth make Radia Perlman the 'Mother of the Internet'. Perlman invented a bridge for sharing data that allowed the Internet to handle massive networks. Perlman holds more than 80 patents related to Internet technology, has won many awards (including being named 1 of the 20 most influential people in her field, twice) and is part of the Internet Hall of Fame.

▲ *Radia Perlman*

1995

Amazon, E-bay and Hotmail arrive on the scene. The Vatican goes online. Chris Lamprecht—a 'minor threat' in Texas, USA—becomes the first person to be banned by a court from accessing the Internet.

1998

Larry Page and Sergey Brin develop a search engine called Backrub—later renamed Google!

2004

Facebook goes online and the world of social networking begins.

2016

Google unveils Google Assistant—a 'smart' voice-activated personal assistant software.

994

irst search e, Yahoo! is ed in April. ping malls ve on the ternet.

HOO!

Networking

Computer networking allows us to collect, organise and share all the knowledge in the world with each other. There are two basic types of networks.

🔍 LAN

Local-area Networks (LANs) connect machines that are close by. This could be in your house, in your school or in an office. The network can be created with wires or fibre-optics. More often, it is done by Ethernet cables or Wi-Fi.

▲ *Network of Ethernet cables at a data centre*

💡 Isn't It Amazing!

In the 1950s, visionary Ted Nelson coined the term 'hyperlink' for the clickable link we see on the web.

🔍 WAN

Wide-area Networks (WANs) connect small networks to larger ones, over entire continents. They use cables, optical fibres and satellites to link up computers. The Internet is the largest WAN.

◀ *Satellite dishes ensure large-scale networking for banks, offices, schools, homes, etc*

👤✓ In Real Life

Machines in a LAN follow rules to "talk" to each other. This is called protocol. For instance, if one device signals "I'm ready to send", it must wait until the other responds "I'm ready to receive." With many computers, protocols become complex, this helps avoid network errors.

Ethernet and Wi-Fi

The most popular system for linking computers is the Ethernet. It was created in 1973 by an American team led by Robert Metcalfe. It became available for public use in 1979.

Wireless technology already existed at this time. But Wi-Fi connectivity came in 1997–1999, after tech experts around the world formed the Wireless Ethernet Compatibility Alliance (WECA).

◄ *Wi-Fi uses a router and radio waves to connect computers to a LAN. The signals can only travel short distances (usually less than 100 metres)*

The World Wide Web and App Stores

The Ethernet became truly useful after the World Wide Web was created. This was done in 1990 by English programmer and physicist Tim Berners-Lee. The web's earliest form had a server, used **HTML** code, and was displayed on the first browser.

In 2009, the mobile phone web came into being. The first one was based on Apple's iTunes. App stores nowadays belong to specific companies. They are run directly on the Internet and are not a part of the World Wide Web.

▶ *Accessing the world through a smartphone has become the modern reality*

The Deep Web

Millions of people around the world use the web for games, news, communication and more. Yet, people are finding it harder and harder to discover data online. This is because only a tiny portion of the World Wide Web is easily accessible. This is called the Surface Web. It is the part of the web that is accessed by search engines like Google. And it only consists of 0.03 per cent of the information that is truly available! The rest of it is buried in the Deep Web. No one really knows how vast the Deep Web is. Our current technology is simply not strong enough to access all of this material. Some part of the Deep Web however is intentionally hidden. This is called the Dark Web.

⊛ Incredible Individuals

In 2009, Chinese-born engineer Charles Kuen Kao received the Nobel Prize in physics, for his discovery, in 1966, of how light can be transmitted through fibre-optic cables. Fibre optics use hair-thin, transparent wires. This forms an alternative to Ethernet in creating LANs.

▲ *Charles Kuen Kao*

The Dark Web

Layers and layers of protection are given to information in the Dark Web. It is often used by criminals as well as government spies to hide their activities. It can only be accessed through special codes or browsers. The special software offers privacy and hides the identity of the user. Thus, it offers security for people who deal with information and goods and services, whether legal or illegal. On the bright side, the Dark Web allows greater freedom to people who live in dictatorial and totalitarian nations. It is also routinely used to leak information about political and organisational wrongdoings, so that powerful but corrupt people are brought to justice.

Artificial Intelligence

Alan Mathison Turing was a British computer scientist who contributed immensely to our knowledge of mathematics, secret codes, logic and philosophy. During World War II, Turing described a machine that could scan its own memory and modify its behaviour. Essentially, it would 'reason' from the information it was given.

▲ *Alan Mathison Turing*

1939

Elektro is the first human-like robot ever seen. He can move his arms and legs, and 'knows' a few jokes.

1941

Author Isaac Asimov describes the Three Laws of Robotics. This is the first known use of the word 'robotics'.

1961

UNIMATE becomes the first mass-produced industrial robot. It looks like a giant arm and weighs over 1800 kilograms.

1960

Computer scientist John McCarthy coins the term **'Artificial Intelligence'**.

1950–1951

Small, wheeled robots like Elsie and Squee are programmed to show 'behaviour'.

1965

DENDRAL is the first AI programme to use a series of 'if-then' rules to make correct decisions.

1976

Inspired by elephant trunks, the Soft Gripper robot gently adjusts its shape to the object it is holding.

The Turing Test

In 1951, Turing created a test for such machines. He proposed that if you cannot tell the difference between answers given by humans and answers given by the machine, then the machine must be thinking. Turing therefore changed the way human beings think about intelligence. Today, Artificial Intelligence or AI can not only learn, reason and solve problems, it can also interact with its surroundings, as we do, and behave accordingly.

1989
AI programme Deep Thought defeats chess master David Levy.

2004
NASA sends two robots—Spirit and Opportunity—to Mars.

2002
Roomba becomes the first robotic vacuum cleaner.

1989
Robotics is now used in military aircrafts. The MQ-1 Predator drone is an unmanned American plane spying over Afghanistan and Pakistan.

2005
AI is used to make self-driving cars.

2000
ASIMO walks, runs and climbs steps like humans. It reacts correctly to human faces and gestures.

1984
The first robot toy, Hero Jr, can play games, sing songs and be your alarm clock. It roams beside you as it 'likes' to stay near humans.

1966
ELIZA can trick people into thinking she is a real doctor!

1999
AIBO—a robotic dog—'learns' and responds to over 100 voice commands. Sometimes, it even ignores you like your real pet!

2011
Siri becomes the first of many AI programmes to be introduced to mobile phones.

Word Check

AM: This stands for Amplitude Modulation, a method in which sound is coded on to radio waves for transmission.

Anode: It is the positively charged electrode by which the electrons leave an electrical device.

Artificial Intelligence: The science of building machines that can imitate human thinking, interactions and responses

Byte: It is a unit of computer information. It is made of 8 bits of data. Other units are given below.

Bit (b) = 0 or 1 unit
1 Byte (B) = 8 bits
1 Kilobyte (KB) = 1024 bytes
1 Megabyte (MB) = 1024 kilobytes
1 Gigabyte (GB) = 1024 megabytes
1 Terabyte (TB) = 1024 gigabytes

Cathode: It is the negatively charged electrode by which electrons enter an electrical device.

Cloud: It is a network of computers and storage devices on the Internet that allows people to store information online.

Electrical conductor: This is any material that allows electricity to flow through it. Most metals fall in this category, while materials like wood, glass and rubber are poor conductors of electricity.

Electromagnetic: It refers to the magnetic field produced by an electric current.

Electron: It is an elementary particle that is negatively charged. The two other elementary particles are protons (which carry a positive charge) and neutrons (which carry no charge at all). Together these three elementary particles form an atom.

FM: Frequency Modulation is a way of imposing sound on to radio waves so they can be transmitted over the radio.

HTML: It is the abbreviation for hypertext markup language: a language that marks up documents for the World Wide Web. It can be used for text, art, sound, video and hyperlinks.

Laser: It is short for Light Amplification by Stimulated Emission of Radiation. Laser is a kind of strong, focussed beam of light.

Matrix: It refers to a close-knit arrangement of elements—like a tight grid or lattice.

Microchip: It is a tiny silicon chip that can be found in many computers. It has electronic circuits that enable the chip to hold information.

Network: It refers to a group of things that are connected to each other in some way.

Photons: It is a particle of light, and a type of electromagnetic radiation.

Radio waves: When electricity and magnetism interact, they produce a variety of wave-like effects called electromagnetic radiation. Many of these waves—radio waves, X-rays, microwaves, infrared rays, ultraviolet rays, gamma rays—are invisible to our eyes. Visible light (all the colours of the rainbow) also consists of electromagnetic waves.

Router: It is a device that allows you to use Wi-Fi by delivering Internet data in a LAN.

Semiconductor: It is a solid substance that is used in electrical devices, as it allows electrical energy and heat to move through it.

Transistor: It is a device that uses semiconductors to control the flow of electricity in a machine.

Vacuum: It is empty space that is free of all matter, even air. It is not possible to have a true and complete vacuum, but you can get very close to it.

Vacuum tube: Also called a valve, this electronic device looks like a light bulb, but works like a switch. When the tube is heated up, it allows electricity to flow through. When the tube is cold, the current stops.